D0771091

SECRETS OF THE ANIMAL WORLD

BEES
Busy Honeymakers

by Eulalia García

Illustrated by Gabriel Casadevall and Ali Garousi

Gareth Stevens Publishing
A WORLD ALMANAC EDUCATION GROUP COMPANY

Please visit our web site at: www.garethstevens.com
For a free color catalog describing Gareth Stevens Publishing's
list of high-quality books and multimedia programs,
call 1-800-542-2595 or fax your request to (414) 332-3567.

The editor would like to extend special thanks to Jan W. Rafert, Curator of Primates
and Small Mammals, Milwaukee County Zoo, Milwaukee, Wisconsin, for his kind
and professional help with the information in this book.

Library of Congress Cataloging-in-Publication Data

García, Eulalia.
   [Abeja. English]
   Bees: busy honeymakers / by Eulalia García; illustrated by Gabriel Casadevall
and Ali Garousi.
      p. cm. – (Secrets of the animal world)
   Includes bibliographical references and index.
   Summary: Describes the physical characteristics, habitat, behavior, and life
cycle of these industrious producers of honey.
   ISBN 0-8368-1634-X (lib. bdg.)
   1. Honeybee–Juvenile literature. [1. Honeybee. 2. Bees.] I. Casadevall,
Gabriel, ill. II. Garousi, Ali, ill. III. Title. IV. Series.
QL568.A6G3713   1997
595.79'9–dc21   97-13053

This North American edition first published in 1997 by
Gareth Stevens Publishing
A World Almanac Education Group Company
330 West Olive Street, Suite 100
Milwaukee, Wisconsin 53212 USA

This U.S. edition © 1997 by Gareth Stevens, Inc. Created with original © 1993
Ediciones Este, S.A., Barcelona, Spain. Additional end matter © 1997 by Gareth
Stevens, Inc.

Series editor: Patricia Lantier-Sampon
Editorial assistants: Diane Laska, Rita Reitci

Printed in the United States of America

2 3 4 5 6 7 8 9 06 05 04 03 02

CONTENTS

THE WORLD OF BEES

Where bees live

Bees are insects grouped with ants and wasps. Only the bee feeds entirely on nectar and pollen. Bees can be solitary or social. The social types form colonies in which each member has a particular task. The honey-producing bees are used in apiculture, or beekeeping. The most common type is the Western honeybee, *Apis mellifera*, a native of Europe, Africa, and Asia. This bee has three female cousins that live only in Asia: the giant honeybee, the size of a large, stinging wasp; the dwarf honeybee, smaller than a fly; and the Oriental hive bee. In temperate climates the hive bee and the honeybee build their hives in hollows of trees as protection from the cold.

Bees collect nectar from flowers and transform it into honey. The honey can be stored for the winter.

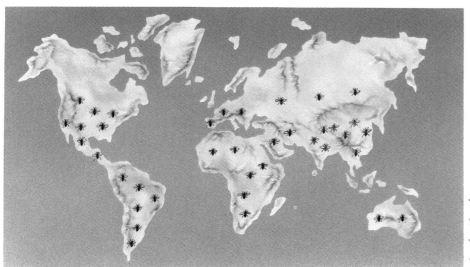

Western honey-bees originated in Asia, but humans brought them around the world. Relatives inhabit India and Southeast Asia.

✳ WESTERN HONEYBEE
✳ GIANT HONEYBEE
✳ DWARF HONEYBEE
✳ ORIENTAL HIVE BEE

Honeybees

Honeybees live in colonies of thousands of individuals that work together for the common good. Each colony has from 30,000 to 60,000 female workers. Young workers clean and warm the breeding cells. Later, they grow glands that produce a nutritious liquid to feed the brood. When these glands are exhausted, the bees grow new glands that produce wax for hive construction. Older workers serve as guards and collectors.

Each colony has a queen bee that relies on the workers to care for her. Drones are the male members of a colony.

Workers in a bee colony are constantly on the move, inspecting the cells, feeding the brood, and maintaining the store of honey so there is enough food to go around.

Each member of a bee colony has a specific job. Bee colonies would be unable to exist if any of its members were missing.

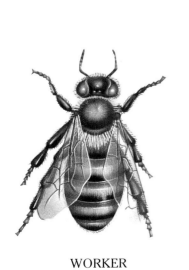

WORKER

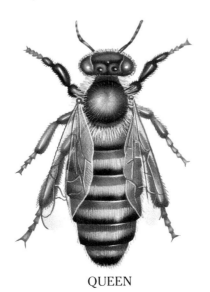

QUEEN

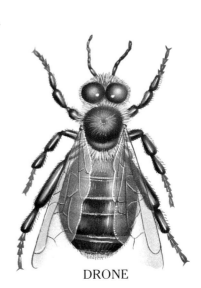

DRONE

Bees and their relatives

Most bees are solitary. Only honeybees and bumblebees are social and live in colonies.

Honeybees set up colonies and store honey all year round in honeycombs. Bumblebees build small, simpler hives. Only the queens survive the winter because they hibernate. When they awaken in spring, they build nests in holes and produce beebread, a mixture of nectar and pollen for the next generation. The queens lay eggs, from which males and workers are born.

Here are a few bee species as well as two of the bees' closest relatives — the ant and the wasp.

LEAF-CUTTING BEE

CARPENTER BEE

WESTERN HONEYBEE

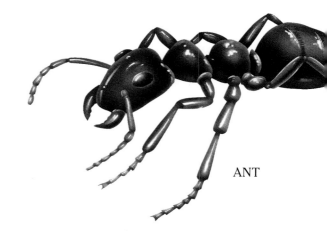

ANT

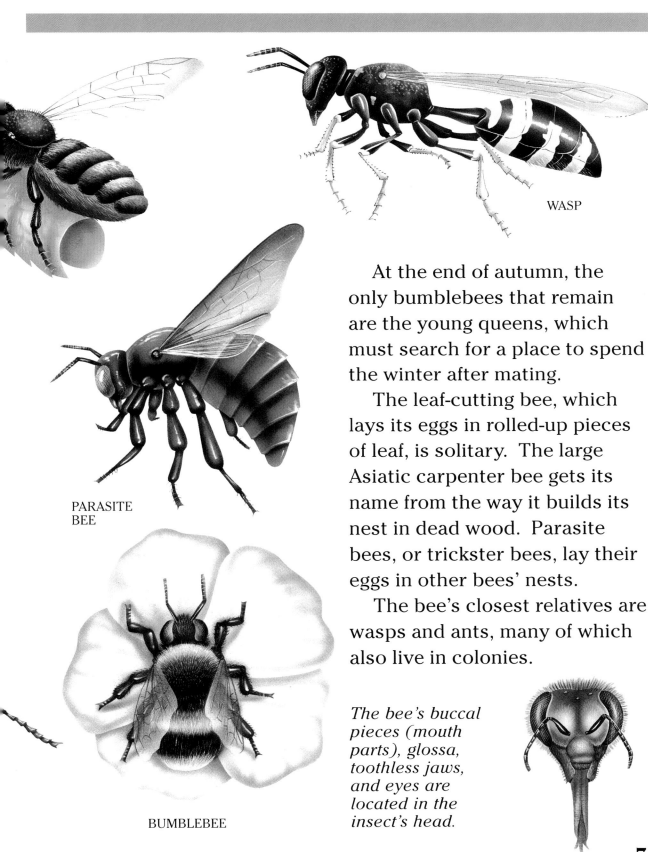

WASP

PARASITE
BEE

BUMBLEBEE

At the end of autumn, the only bumblebees that remain are the young queens, which must search for a place to spend the winter after mating.

The leaf-cutting bee, which lays its eggs in rolled-up pieces of leaf, is solitary. The large Asiatic carpenter bee gets its name from the way it builds its nest in dead wood. Parasite bees, or trickster bees, lay their eggs in other bees' nests.

The bee's closest relatives are wasps and ants, many of which also live in colonies.

The bee's buccal pieces (mouth parts), glossa, toothless jaws, and eyes are located in the insect's head.

7

INSIDE THE BEE

Bees are small insects with an external skeleton, jointed legs, and a segmented body. The bee's body has three parts: the head, with its buccal parts, antennae, and five eyes; the thorax, to which its six legs are connected; and the abdomen, which contains most of the digestive tract and wax glands.

PHARYNGEAL GLANDS
Present in workers only, these glands work for about ten days. They produce royal jelly to feed the queen and royal larvae. Other larvae get royal jelly only during the first three days of life.

FLIGHT MUSCLES

NERVOUS SYSTEM

THORAX

ESOPHAGUS

BRAIN

COMPOUND EYES
Each eye is formed of thousands of little eyes set side by side. They do not see as sharply as human eyes, but they can detect very rapid movements.

PHARYNX
Acts as a pump to bring up liquids that are then sent into the honey sac.

ANTENNA

HEAD

JAWS
Used for cutting and molding wax, opening pollen sacs in flowers, collecting pollen, and removing dead larvae and dirt from the hive.

GLOSSA
Used by the worker to suck up nectar from flowers. To eat some solids, the bee has to first dampen the food with saliva. The glossa of the queen and drone are much shorter.

LEG

CLAWS

8

HONEY SAC
An expandable sac that holds nectar collected by a worker, to be regurgitated when the bee returns to the hive. If hungry, a bee can release some into its stomach.

INTESTINE
A short part of the digestive tract ending in a baglike rectum, which accumulates body waste during winter and expels it in spring.

WINGS
The bee folds its four transparent wings on its back when resting. When the bee flies, its wings move as if they were one pair. This is because a row of small hooks on the back wings connects them to the front wings.

STOMACH

HEART
The bee's heart is a tube with five chambers. These chambers contract to distribute blood through the body, either through vessels or by flooding.

ABDOMEN

AIR SACS
Instead of lungs, bees have several elastic tubes that open up to the exterior through twenty holes, called spiracles. Connected to these tubes are the air sacs. Air moves through the tubes and air sacs to provide the bee with respiration.

RECTUM

ANUS

SPIRACLE

WAX GLANDS
Bees produce wax to build honeycombs. The wax leaves the bee's body in sheets through the bottom of the abdomen. These sheets are then kneaded in the mouth and formed into cells.

POISON SAC

OVARIES
The ovaries of worker bees do not function. Queen bees can use them their entire lives. The queen normally mates only once a year and can lay about two thousand eggs a day.

STINGER
The stinger's tip has barbs. When a bee stings, it injects a poison that can be deadly for some insects. Only female bees sting.

BEES — HONEY PRODUCERS

Making honey

Flowers produce a sugary liquid called nectar that attracts worker bees, flies, beetles, and many other insects. Only bees can transform nectar into honey.

Bees visit flowers to collect drops of nectar. The human stomach transforms food into nutrients to form essential body tissues. In bees, only a small portion goes into the stomach. The rest is kept in the honey sac and taken back to the hive.

Honey production begins when the bee collects the first drops of nectar. The bee mixes these drops with its saliva before returning to the hive.

Foraging bees deliver honey to worker bees in the hive. The workers swallow and mix it with saliva. They regurgitate and store the honey in open cells so that it loses its water. This thickens the honey. Then the workers seal the cells with wax.

Recently collected nectar passes from one worker's mouth to another to produce honey that is stored and left to evaporate in the hive's cells.

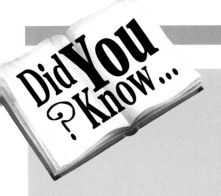

that bees carry "saddlebags?"

Foraging bees do not swallow pollen as they do nectar. Instead, they carry it back to the hive in baskets, or saddlebags, attached to their legs.

Pollen sticks to the hairs of the worker's body. The worker combs the pollen from the hairs into baskets on its legs. These baskets, or saddlebags, are made of long, curved hairs on the hind legs. The bee packs the pollen firmly in its baskets.

When the worker returns to the hive, it leaves the load in cells reserved for pollen.

The honey dance

Before collecting nectar, worker bees fly in circles, gradually getting farther from the hive, to keep track of their position. When they find flowers rich in sun. When it is cloudy, they use polarized light to find their way. To guide other workers to the flowers, the bee performs two types of dances in the dark interior of the hive.

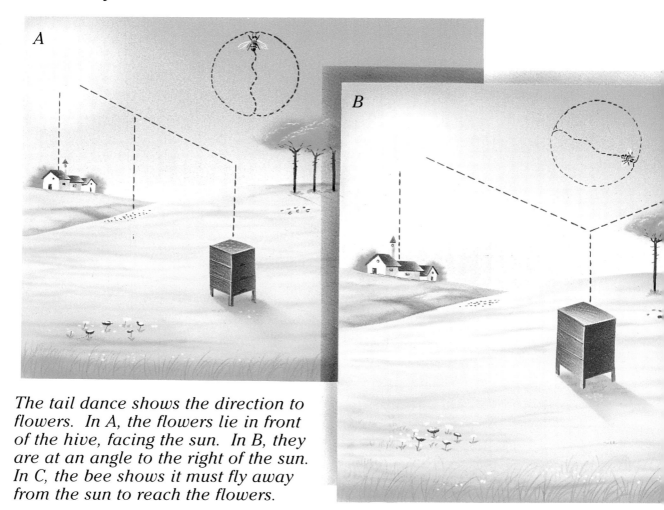

The tail dance shows the direction to flowers. In A, the flowers lie in front of the hive, facing the sun. In B, they are at an angle to the right of the sun. In C, the bee shows it must fly away from the sun to reach the flowers.

nectar, they fly back to the hive to inform the others. The bees never lose their way because they fly by the position of the

One is a circular dance, which indicates that food is near — at less than 80 feet (25 meters). The other dance the bee performs consists of shaking its abdomen. This is called the tail dance and indicates the distance and direction of the flowers according to the angle from the sun. The rate of shaking indicates distance; the fewer shakes, the greater the distance.

The bee never moves its abdomen while performing the circular dance. It shakes its abdomen only to explain the distance the other bees must take to reach the flowers.

CIRCULAR DANCE   TAIL DANCE

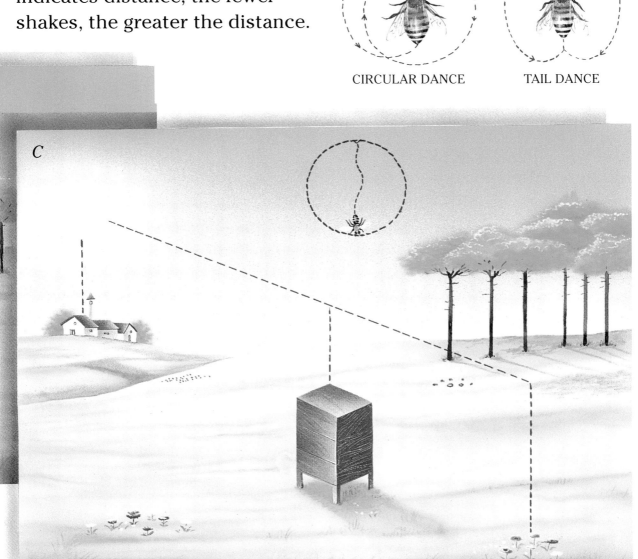

C

BEES AND HONEY

The honeycomb

Bees store honey and pollen in the cells of the honeycomb, which also houses the brood. On each side of a thin wall of wax, the bees construct the cells, placed at a slight angle to prevent the contents from sliding out.

Each cell is hexagonal in shape, except for the royal cells, which are the same shape as a peanut. Bees build hexagonal cells because they fit together perfectly, with no wasted space between the cells.

Hexagonal cells are used both as storehouses for pollen and nectar and as rooms for the young. This worker is leaving a cell after completing its work.

Worker bees construct comb only during the one time their wax glands function. This period lasts from two to eight days.

that drones die after mating with the queen?

Of all the females in the hive, only queens mate. On sunny days, when there is no wind, mating takes place in mid-flight. This is called the nuptial flight. Every year, drones gather in the open to wait for new young queens. When one arrives, the new queen may mate with six to twelve drones. The queen then returns to her hive and spends her life laying eggs. The mating drones die immediately. In the fall, the workers drive the remaining drones out of the hive to die of starvation.

Collecting honey

For every pound (.5 kg) of honey, bees must make more than 25,000 flights to millions of flowers to collect enough nectar.

From the beginning of summer to the start of fall, beekeepers collect honey that is produced in wooden boxes along a thin sheet of artificial wax upon which bees construct honeycombs. When the combs are full of honey, the beekeepers remove some of them, leaving enough to feed the bees. Beekeepers must be careful to see that the queen and the brood remain in the hive, since they are the source of future honey production. The queen

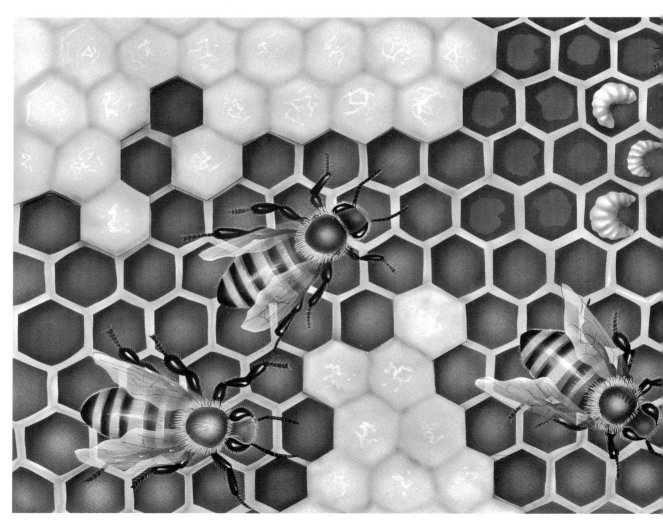

always lays her eggs near the center of the hive. Around each group of eggs, workers fill other cells with pollen and place honey on the outer wall of the honeycomb. Beekeepers collect the honey by smoking the bees. Smoke makes the bees eat lots of honey, and they become so full they cannot sting.

Right: Beekeepers use special hives for their bees. They are made of wooden boxes with movable frames in which the bees make their honeycomb.

Below, left: This honeycomb contains mature honey, unborn workers, and young drones.

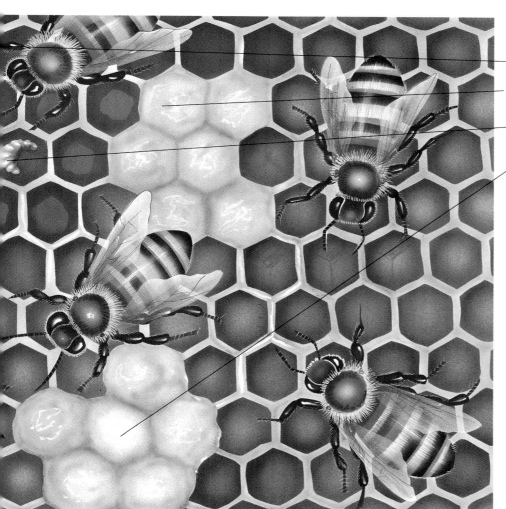

MATURE HONEY CELLS

POLLEN CELLS

WORKER LARVAE

DRONE CELLS

Below: Some cells of the honeycomb contain young larvae.

BEES AND EVOLUTION

From solitary to social

The first bees probably looked like carnivorous wasps that changed to a diet of nectar and pollen about 135 to 65 million years ago, soon after flowers appeared on Earth.

Scientists can trace how bees evolved from ancient, simple societies to modern, complex ones. Most bees that build nests and lay eggs die long before the larvae hatch. The first eggs of bumblebees consist of weak, sterile females that become helpers of the stronger queens.

Bees communicate in several ways. The easiest way to indicate where nectar is located is to accompany the other bees to the site, a common method used by stingless bees. Dwarf honeybees communicate by flying in circles or shaking the abdomen, but only in daytime. Only Oriental hive and Western honeybees can point out precise directions inside the dark hive.

A bumblebee's nest, made of moss. Inside are the queen, a few cells, and a small store of food.

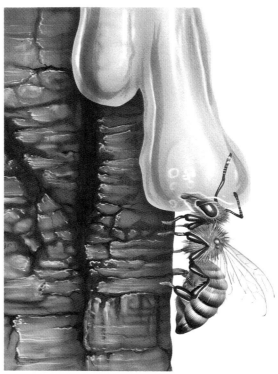

Millions of years ago, thousands of insects like this bee became trapped in the resin of pine trees that grew on Earth at the time.

Did **You** ? Know...

that bees can smell with their antennae?

For a bee, losing the sense of smell would be disastrous. Inside the dark hive, bees guide themselves by touch and odor.

The bee does not have a nose. Its sense of smell is located in its antennae. The antennae look like two movable sticks with jointed segments. All antennae have tiny points that are sensitive to odor.

Using their antennae, bees can recognize each other in the darkness of the hive and even warn each other of an intruder's presence.

HOW BEES BEHAVE

A city of bees

The queen lays the hive's eggs. Drones and workers hatch as larvae that, in a process called metamorphosis, change into pupae, then adults. The queen lays fertilized eggs that produce females and unfertilized eggs that produce males. Whether fertilized eggs are workers or queens depends on the size of their cell and the food they eat.

The queen emits a smell that attracts workers. As the queen gets old, the smell becomes

Bees communicate through smell. This worker is calling its companions by using its odor glands.

weaker until it disappears. Workers notice this and build several royal cells to make sure there will be a new queen.

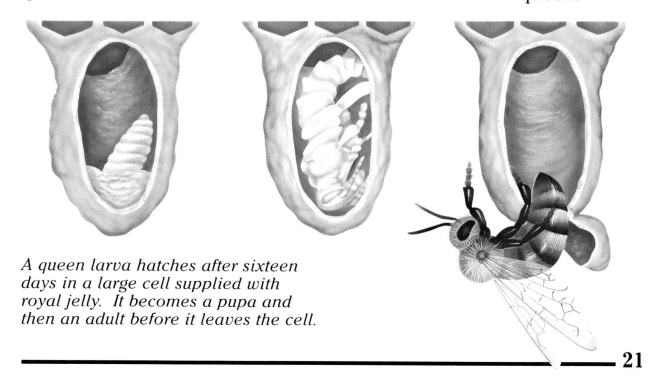

A queen larva hatches after sixteen days in a large cell supplied with royal jelly. It becomes a pupa and then an adult before it leaves the cell.

Establishing a hive

In spring, when flowers are full of nectar, bees prepare to swarm, or leave the old hive to form new colonies. First, the workers rear six or more queens, feeding the larvae royal jelly instead of the usual honey and pollen. Before the old queen leaves, a group of drones waits at the hive entrance with stomachs full of honey. As they leave, they form a swarm that follows the old queen. When the queen stops, so do the workers. Explorers then look for a new home.

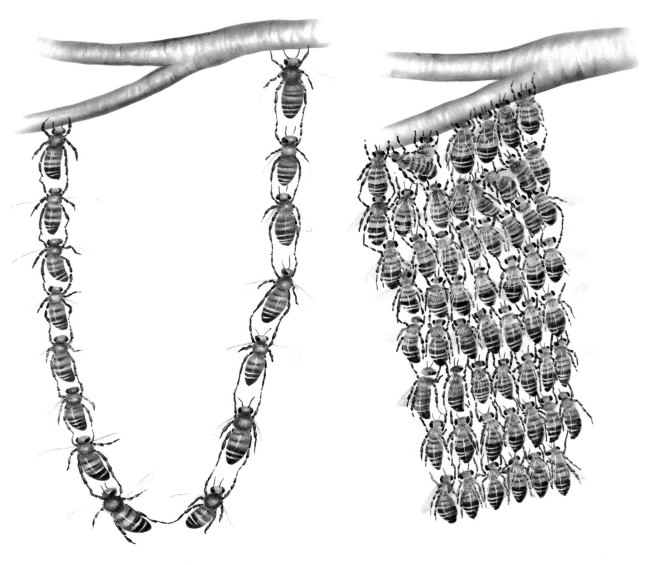

In the old hive, if the workers decide to form only a single swarm, the first queen to leave a royal cell stings the others while they are still inside their cells.

If two queens emerge at the same time, they fight until one is killed.

The queen lays one egg in each cell after making sure the cell is clean.

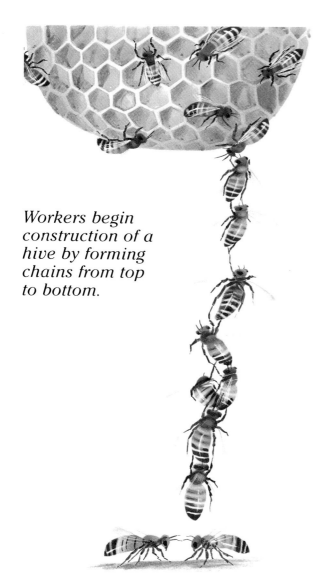

Workers begin construction of a hive by forming chains from top to bottom.

If the workers decide to build more colonies, they defend the royal cells from the attack of the first queen. The future queens remain in their cells until this queen leaves with her swarm.

Then another new queen emerges from a cell, and the others die. This new queen mates with several drones. After mating, the queen returns to her hive to lay eggs.

APPENDIX TO

SECRETS
OF THE
ANIMAL WORLD

BEES
Busy Honeymakers

BEE SECRETS

▼ **Bee enemies.** The bee has many enemies. Some animals attack the hives and eat the food stores. Others prey on the bees as they collect honey.

How long can a honeybee live? A queen bee can live up to four or five years. Drones hatch only in spring and usually live until the fall.

Workers can live up to six months if they hatch in the fall, but only several weeks if they hatch in the spring. Because the spring season is when there is most work to do, these workers age very quickly.

▲ **The double-edged sting.** Bees will die after stinging mammals because the stinger remains buried in its victim. When the bee tries to pull it out, it loses part of its abdomen and dies. If it stings another insect, it can remove its stinger cleanly.

▼ **Illnesses.** One of the illnesses feared by beekeepers is caused by the tiny acarus mite, which feeds on the internal juices of bees.

The color of flowers. Bees, unlike humans, cannot tell the difference between colors. This is because they only see ultraviolet light, which humans cannot see. A flower that appears totally white to humans is blue to bees, and what is red for us is a blackish tone for bees.

▶ **Air conditioning and central heating.** When it is very hot, worker bees beat their wings rapidly to cool the hive. When it gets very cold in winter, the workers bunch together and produce heat by making their muscles vibrate.

1. What do workers do during their first few days of life?
   a) Become guards and collectors.
   b) Clean and heat up the cells.
   c) Build cells.

2. Which members of the hive have a stinger?
   a) The females.
   b) Only the drones.
   c) Only the queen.

3. What do the pharyngeal glands secrete?
   a) Wax.
   b) Royal jelly.
   c) Saliva.

4. How do workers carry pollen?
   a) In small hair baskets on the legs.
   b) In their stomachs.
   c) Between their legs.

5. What does a bee's circular dance mean?
   a) The nectar is very far away.
   b) There is a lot of nectar.
   c) The nectar is less than 80 feet (25 m) away.

6. How does the beekeeper quiet the bees when collecting honey?
   a) By giving them sugar water.
   b) By applying smoke to the hive.
   c) By collecting only at night.

The answers to BEE SECRETS questions are on page 32.

GLOSSARY

accumulate: to gather or collect a large amount of something.

apiculture: the keeping of bees in order to collect the honey.

barb: a sharp point sticking out backward to prevent something coming out easily.

beebread: a mixture of nectar and pollen made by bees as a protein source to feed young and adult bees.

breeding cells: honeycomb cells used for rearing young bees.

brood: a group of young reared at the same time.

buccal pieces: structures of or very close to the mouth.

carnivorous: meat-eating.

colony: a group or community where all members work or live together.

elastic: able to stretch easily and go back to a former shape.

emerge: to appear or show up suddenly out of something.

emit: to send forth or give out.

essential: something that cannot be done without.

evaporate: to give off moisture.

evolve: to change shape or develop gradually from one form to another over time.

forage: to search for food.

generation: a group of animals, plants, or humans of about the same general age.

glands: organs in the body that make and release substances such as sweat, tears, saliva, and poison.

glossa: the long feeding tube, or tongue, located on or under the head of some insects. The bee sucks up nectar through its glossa.

hexagonal: having six sides.

hibernate: to enter a state of rest or inactivity, usually for the winter season.

larva: the wingless, wormlike form of a newly-hatched insect; the stage of life that comes after the egg but before full development.

mammals: warm-blooded animals

that have backbones and hair. Female mammals produce milk to feed their young.

mate: to join together (animals) to produce young.

metamorphosis: a complete change in form or appearance; in most insects, this change occurs in stages: egg, larva, pupa, and adult.

nectar: a sweet liquid found in many flowers that is often used as a food source by insects.

nuptial flight: a stage in the bee's breeding cycle when male bees, or drones, and their queen fly away from the hive and mate.

nutrients: the elements in food that help a plant or animal grow and develop.

nutritious: capable of helping the growth and development of plants and animals.

ovaries: the parts of female animals or plants that produce eggs.

parasite: a plant or animal that lives in or on another plant or animal.

pharyngeal glands: glands in the region of the worker bee's pharynx that produce royal jelly to feed to larvae. After ten days, these glands no longer work.

pharynx: the part of the throat just behind the mouth.

polarized light: light waves vibrating in a definite direction.

pollen: fine yellow dust from a plant, made up of particles that develop into male cells that enable a female plant's ovaries to produce seeds. Bees use pollen as a protein food source.

pupa: The third life-cycle stage of most insects, between larva and adult.

regurgitate: to bring something back up through the throat after it has been swallowed; to vomit.

resin: a yellow or brown sticky liquid that oozes from certain trees.

respiration: the act of breathing; providing oxygen to the body.

royal jelly: a highly nutritious substance made by the bee's pharyngeal glands, which is fed to very young larvae and all queen larvae.

sac: a part of a plant or animal that is like a bag or pouch.

saliva: the fluid made by glands in the mouth to keep the mouth moist and to help in chewing, swallowing, and digesting food. The bee also uses saliva to help change nectar into honey.

segmented: divided into sections. A bee's body is divided into three segments.

solitary: living alone; isolated.

sperm: the male reproductive cell.

swarm: a large number of insects that travel together.

transform: to change in form or appearance.

transparent: allowing light to pass through so that objects on the inside or other side can be seen clearly.

ultraviolet light: light rays in a range that humans cannot see.

ACTIVITIES

◆ Some museums and nature centers keep demonstration beehives made of clear plastic or glass. Visit such a hive if you can. Select a half dozen individual bees and follow the movements of each one, keeping notes of what it does. Can you tell from the bee's actions if it is a worker or a drone? What special job does the worker bee you study seem to have? Does it tend the larvae, fly out to bring back honey, or guard the nest? How do the bees seem to cooperate to get the hive's work done?

◆ Visit a beekeeper in your area to find out how bees can be kept. How is the honey harvested and prepared for human consumption? Do the bees help pollinate crops? How does the beekeeper help the bees survive winter when they cannot gather nectar? What kind of diseases or pests must the beekeeper watch out for? How does the keeper keep his bees healthy? How does the beekeeper keep his bees when they want to swarm and start a new colony?

MORE BOOKS TO READ

A Beekeeper's Year. Sylvia A. Johnson (Little, Brown)
Bees. The New Creepy Crawly Collection. Enid Fisher (Gareth Stevens)
Busy Bees. Bronwen Scarffe (SRA School Group)
A Day in the Life of a Beekeeper. P. Michaels and J. Tropea (Troll)
The Fascinating World of Bees. J. M. Parramon (Barron)
The Honeybee in the Meadow. Christopher O'Toole (Gareth Stevens)
Honeybees at Home. Lynne Harwood (Tilbury House)
Killer Bees. Kathleen Davis and Dave Mayes (Silver Burdett)
Wasps at Home. Bianca Lavies (Dutton Children's Books)
The World of Honeybees. Virginia Harrison (Gareth Stevens)
Yellowjackets. Edward S. Ross (Child's World)

VIDEOS

The Bee. (Barr Films)
Bee Basics. (Pyramid Film and Video)
Bees. (Phoenix/BFA Films and Video)
The Honeybee. (Encyclopædia Britannica Educational Corporation)
The Wasp. (Barr Films)

PLACES TO VISIT

Cincinnati Zoo Insect World
3400 Vine Street
Cincinnati, OH 45220

Australian Museum
6 - 8 College Street
Sydney, NSW
Australia 2000

Auckland Institute and Museum
Auckland, New Zealand

Otto Orkin Insect Zoo National Museum of Natural History
Smithsonian Institution
10 Constitution Avenue
Washington, DC 20560

Metropolitan Toronto Zoo
Meadowvale Road,
    West Hill
Toronto, Ontario M1E 4R5

Museum of Victoria
222 Exhibition Street
Melbourne, Victoria
Australia 3000

Calgary Zoo
1300 Zoo Road
Calgary, Alberta
T2V 7E6

INDEX

**Answers to
BEE SECRETS
questions:**
1. **b**
2. **a**
3. **b**
4. **a**
5. **c**
6. **b**